THIN BLUE LINES

THIN BLUE LINES

Cartoons for the United Nations

Edited by Mark Bryant

LEO COOPER
LONDON

First published in Great Britain in 1995 by
Leo Cooper Ltd, 190 Shaftesbury Avenue, London WC2H 8JL
an imprint of
Pen & Sword Books Ltd
47 Church Street, Barnsley, South Yorkshire, S70 2AS

A CIP record of this book is available from the British Library

ISBN 0 85052 466 0

Acknowledgements

For their kind permission to use cartoons in this book, the United Nations
Association and the publishers would like to thank the following:

Basler Zeitung, Cartoonist, Daily Mail, Daily Mirror, Daily Star, European,
Farworks Inc/Universal Press Syndicate, *Financial Times, Guardian,*
Independent, Independent Magazine, Independent on Sunday, Macmillan
Publishers, *Marine Pollution Bulletin, Nursing Times, Private Eye, Punch,*
Telegraph Magazine, The Times

Printed by Redwood Books Ltd
Trowbridge, Wiltshire

Preface

1995 marks the fiftieth anniversary of the United Nations and this book, tied in with an exhibition and auction of the drawings, is part of a nationwide celebration of the UN's achievements since the end of the Second World War. All royalties from sales of this book and all proceeds of the auction go to the United Nations Association.

Interspersed with cartoons donated by some of the very best artists working today are 50 brief statements of what the various organizations within the United Nations have accomplished over the past five decades. However, it should be stressed that the cartoons printed with these boxed items were not specifically drawn to illustrate them, but were selected from the many cartoons submitted, where they seemed appropriate.

Thanks are due to all those cartoonists whose generosity has made this book and the auction possible, and also to the editors of the various newspapers and magazines in which some of the cartoons first appeared.

Special thanks also go to all who have helped in the preparation of this book, in particular Sir Hugh Rossi, John MacOmish, Christopher Birks, Christel Kaestner and Tony Samphier of the United Nations Association; Leo Cooper and Georgina Harris of Leo Cooper Limited; and Joanna Lumley for kindly agreeing to write the Foreword. **M.B.**

Foreword

This year sees the 50th Anniversary of the United Nations Association. For some years now I have been privileged to have my name linked with the Association as an 'ambassadress'. I cannot say that my duties have been onerous but if, by helping in any way that I can, I can make the public more aware of the work of the Association and indeed the United Nations itself, I shall be happy.

It is perhaps particularly ironic that when I agreed to lend my name to help publicise this book all was Quiet on the Western Front, so to speak. It is perhaps an odd thing now to be celebrating the Anniversary with a book of cartoons — when on the other hand the United Nations can be seen taking an evermore active role in the conflict in former Yugoslavia. Seldom has the role of the United Nations enjoyed a higher profile. Let this not obscure all the other activities in which the Association is currently involved and let us also take the opportunity to laugh amongst ourselves at some of the ingenious and often moving drawings displayed by all the talented contributors to this book. Without a sense of humour, none of us would survive for very long.

Joanna Lumley
OCTOBER 1995

Index of Artists

For heaven's sake, if the whole United Nations can enjoy their fiftieth — why not you?

Maintaining peace and security. By deploying more than 35 peacekeeping forces and observer missions, the United Nations has been able to restore calm to allow the negotiating process to go forward while saving millions of people from becoming casualties of conflicts. There are presently 16 active peacekeeping forces in operation.

4

Bloody magnolia again!

Making peace. Since 1945, the United Nations has been credited with negotiating 172 peaceful settlements that have ended regional conflicts. Recent cases include an end to the Iran-Iraq war, the withdrawal of Soviet troops from Afghanistan, and an end to the civil war in El Salvador. The United Nations has used quiet diplomacy to avert over 80 imminent wars.

Don't take it so hard, Mr Tanaka. We've *all* lost priceless bonsai to acid rain

Promoting democracy. The United Nations has enabled people in over 45 countries to participate in free and fair elections, including those held in Cambodia, Namibia, El Salvador, Eritrea, Mozambique, Nicaragua and South Africa. It has provided electoral advice, assistance, and monitoring of results.

8

Promoting development. The UN system has devoted more attention and resources to the promotion of the development of human skills and potentials than any other external assistance effort. The system's annual disbursements, including loans and grants, amount to more than $10 billion. The UN Development Programme (UNDP), in close cooperation with over 170 Member States and other UN agencies, designs and implements projects for agriculture, industry, education, and the environment. It supports more than 5,000 projects with a budget of $1.3 billion. It is the largest multilateral source of grant development assistance. The World Bank, at the forefront in mobilizing support for developing countries worldwide, has alone loaned $333 billion for development projects since 1946. In addition, UNICEF spends more than $800 million a year primarily on immunization, health care, nutrition and basic education in 138 countries.

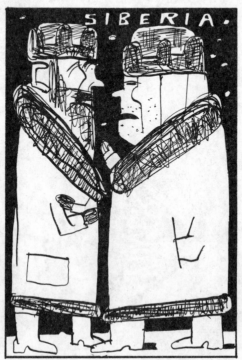

So you're being released? Neither am I

Promoting human rights. Since adopting the Universal Declaration of Human Rights in 1948, the United Nations has helped enact more than 80 comprehensive agreements on political, civil, economic, social and cultural rights. By investigating individual complaints of human rights abuses, the UN Human Rights Commission has focused world attention on cases of torture, disappearance, and arbitrary detention and has generated international pressure to be brought on governments to improve their human rights records.

Protecting the environment. The United Nations has played a vital role in fashioning a global programme designed to protect the environment. The 'Earth Summit', the UN Conference on Environment Development held in Rio de Janeiro in 1992, resulted in treaties on bio-diversity and climate change, and all countries adopted 'Agenda 21' – a blueprint to promote sustainable development or the concept of economic growth while protecting natural resources.

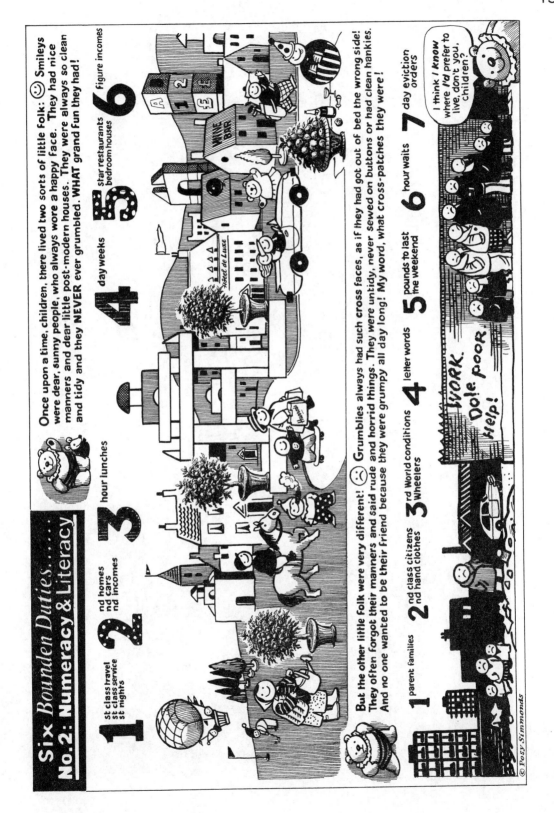

ROY DAVIS

Preventing nuclear proliferation. The United Nations, through the International Atomic Energy Agency, has helped minimize the threat of nuclear war by inspecting nuclear reactors in 90 countries to ensure that nuclear materials are not diverted for military purposes.

Underarms Limitation

Promoting self-determination and independence. The United Nations has played a pivotal role in bringing about independence in 80 countries that are now among its Member States.

It's a jungle out there

Strengthening international law. Over 300 international treaties, on topics as varied as human rights conventions to agreements on the use of outer space and the seabed, have been enacted through the efforts of the United Nations.

Drennan

Drat! It's that crackpot lawman again!

Have you any idea why the kids have taken to wearing these blue berets?

Let's get out of here — the canary's dead!

Handing down judicial settlements of major international disputes. By giving judgements and advisory opinions, the International Court of Justice has helped settle international disputes involving territorial issues, non-interference in the internal affairs of states, diplomatic relations, hostage-taking, the right of asylum, rights of passage and economic rights.

They've agreed to remove the roadblock — and the colonel's shaking hands on it right now

Ending apartheid in South Africa. By imposing measures ranging from an arms embargo to a convention against segregated sporting events, the United Nations was a major factor in bringing about the downfall of the apartheid system, which the General Assembly called 'a crime against humanity'. Elections were held in April 1994 in which all South Africans were allowed to participate on an equal basis, following the establishment of a majority government.

Why do we fight? We fight so that all our people will be free. Also, it beats being an unemployed garden-furniture salesman...

1, 2, 3, 4, 5 – once I caught a fish alive...

Apparently, at the end of the day they all change into designer suits and drive home in new cars

Aiding Palestinian refugees. Since 1950, the United Nations Relief and Works Agency (UNRWA) has sustained four generations of Palestinians with free schooling, essential health care, relief assistance and key social services virtually without interruption. There are 2.9 million refugees in the Middle East served by UNRWA.

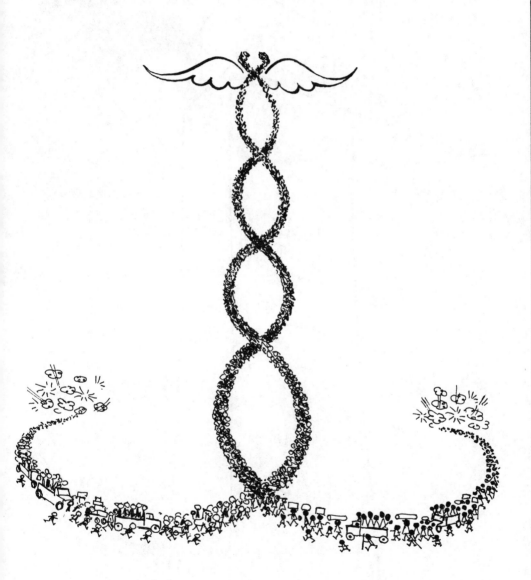

ROY DAVIS

Providing humanitarian aid to victims of conflict. More than 30 million refugees fleeing war, famine or persecution have received aid from the UN High Commissioner for Refugees since 1951 in a continuing effort coordinated by the United Nations that often involves other agencies. There are more than 19 million refugees, primarily women and children, who are receiving food, shelter, medical aid, education and repatriation assistance.

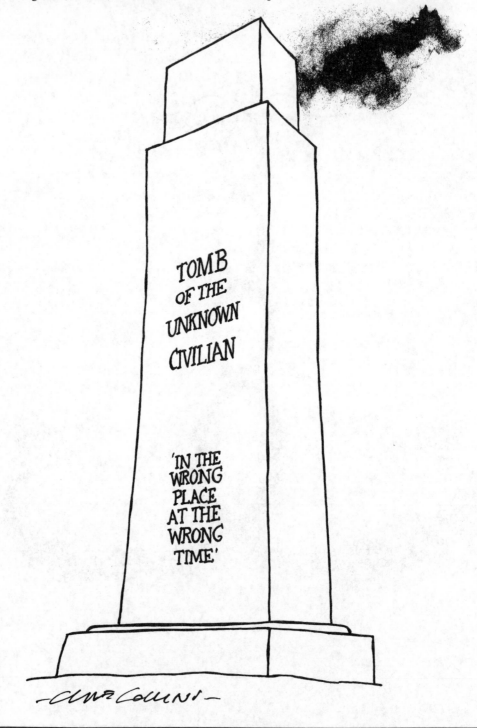

Alleviating chronic hunger and rural poverty in developing countries. The International Fund for Agricultural Development (IFAD) has developed a system of providing credit, often in very small amounts, for the poorest and most marginalized groups that has benefited over 230 million people in nearly 100 developing countries.

Focusing on African development. For the United Nations' Africa continues to be the highest priority. In 1986, the United Nations convened a special session to drum up international support for African economic recovery and development. The United Nations has also instituted a system-wide task force to ensure that commitments made by the international community are honoured and challenges met. The Africa Project Development Facility has helped entrepreneurs in 25 countries to find financing for new enterprises. The Facility has completed 130 projects which represent investments of $233 million and the creation of 13,000 new jobs. It is expected that these new enterprises will either earn or save some $131 million in foreign exchange annually.

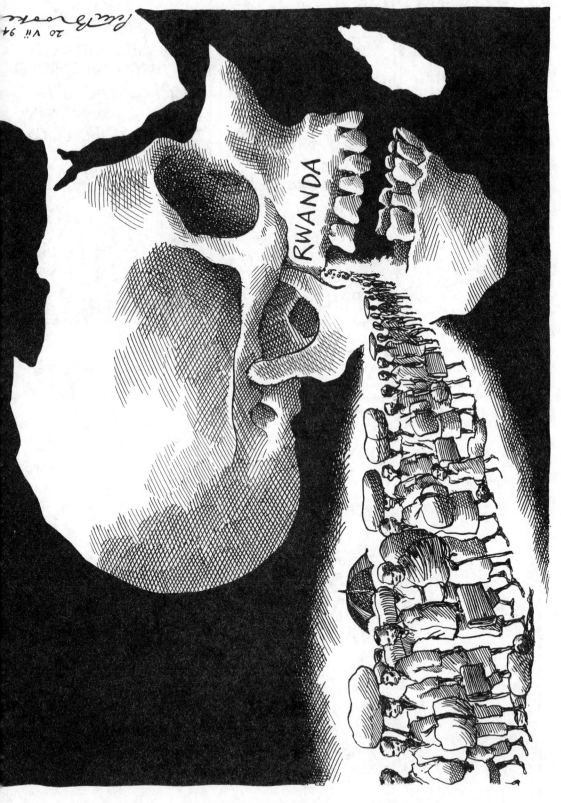

Out of Rwanda

Eurocats

Promoting women's rights. A long-term objective of the United Nations has been to improve the lives of women and to empower women to have greater control over their lives. Several conferences during the UN-sponsored International Women's Decade set an agenda for the advancement of women and women's rights for the rest of the century. The UN Development Fund for Women (UNIFEM) and the International Research and Training Institute for the Advancement of Women (INSTRAW) have supported programmes and projects to improve the quality of life for women in over 100 countries. They include credit and training, access to new food-production technologies and marketing opportunites, and other means of promoting women's work.

Kipper Williams

Providing safe drinking-water. UN agencies have worked to make safe drinking-water available to 1.3 billion people in rural areas during the last decade.

32

Eradicating smallpox. A 13-year effort by the World Health Organization resulted in the complete eradication of smallpox from the planet in 1980. The eradication has saved an estimated $1 billion a year in vaccination and monitoring, almost three times the cost of elimating the scourge itself. WHO also helped wipe out polio from the Western hemisphere, with global eradication expected by the year 2000.

From here I can see the need for five UN Peacekeeping Missions

Pressing for universal immunization. Polio, tetanus, measles, whooping-cough, diphtheria and tuberculosis still kill more than 8 million children each year. In 1974, only 5 per cent of children in developing countries were immunized against these diseases. Today, as a result of the efforts of UNICEF and WHO, there is an 80 per cent immunization rate, saving the lives of more than 3 million children each year.

36

Do you do a bankrupt businessman special?

Reducing child mortality rates. Through oral rehydration therapy, water and sanitation and other health and nutrition measures undertaken by UN agencies, child mortality rates in the developing countries have been halved since 1960, increasing the average life expectancy from 37 to 67 years.

Fighting parasitic diseases. Efforts by UN agencies in North Africa to eliminate the dreaded screw-worm, a parasite that feeds on human and animal flesh, prevented the spread of the parasite, which is carried by flies, to Egypt, Tunisia, sub-Saharan Africa and Europe. A WHO programme has also saved the lives of 7 million children from going blind from river blindness and rescued many others from guinea-worm and other tropical diseases.

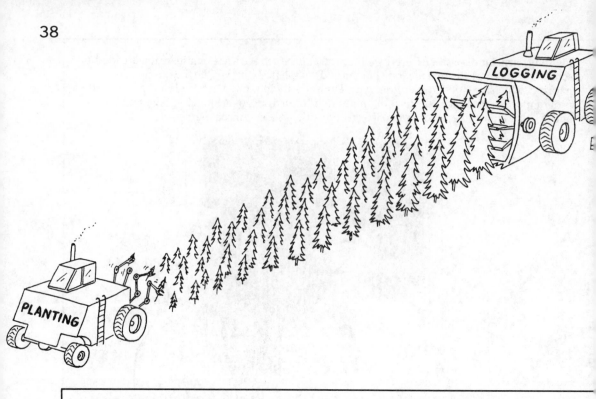

Promoting investment in developing countries. The United Nations, through the efforts of the UN Industrial Development Organization (UNIDO), has served as a 'match-maker' for North-South, South-South and East-West investment, promoting entrepreneurship and self-reliance, industrial cooperation and technology transfer and cost-effective, ecologically sensitive industry.

Stop that, man. You're a disgrace to your uniform

Orienting economic policy towards social need. Many UN agencies have emphasized the need to take account of human needs in determining economic adjustment and restructuring policies and programmes, including measures to safeguard the poor, especially in areas of health and education, and 'debt swaps for children'.

I hated my dove-of-peace image

Reducing the effects of natural disasters. The World Meteorological Organization (WMO) has spared millions of people from the calamitous effects of both natural and man-made disasters. Its early warning system, which utilizes thousands of surface monitors as well as satellites, has provided information for the dispersal of oil spills and has predicted long-term droughts. The system has allowed for the efficient distribution of food aid to drought regions, such as southern Africa in 1992.

I've heard of freak storms raining fishes and frogs before, but...

Providing food to victims of emergencies. Over two million tons of food are distributed each year by the World Food Programme (WFP). Nearly 30 million people facing acute food shortages in 36 countries benefited from this assistance in 1994.

Clearing land mines. The United Nations is leading an international effort to clear land mines from former battlefields in Afghanistan, Angola, Cambodia, El Salvador, Mozambique, Rwanda and Somalia that still kill and maim thousands of innocent people every year.

What do you reckon our chances are of getting home for the fiftieth anniversary celebrations?

44

Protecting the ozone layer. The UN Environment Programme (UNEP) and the World Meteorological Organization (WMO) have been instrumental in highlighting the damage caused to the earth's ozone layer. As a result of a treaty, known as the Montreal Protocol, there has been a global effort to reduce chemical emissions of substances that have caused the depletion of the ozone layer. The effort will spare millions of people from the increased risk of contracting cancer due to additional exposure to ultraviolet radiation.

Just how big do you reckon this hole in the ozone layer is, Norman?

Curbing global warming. Through the Global Environment Facility, countries have contributed substantial resources to curb conditions that cause global warming. Increasing emissions from burning fossil fuels and changes in land-use patterns have led to a build-up of gases in the atmosphere, which experts believe can lead to a warming of the Earth's temperature.

46

General Dynamics

We're having to diversify

Preventing over-fishing. The Food and Agriculture Organization (FAO) monitors marine fishery production and issues alerts to prevent damage due to over-fishing.

GLASS BOTTOMED BOAT

47

Wherever she went crowds of street urchins would follow.

KUT-UPS

Limiting deforestation and promoting sustainable forestry development. FAO, UNDP and the World Bank, through a Tropical Forests Action Programme, have formulated and carried out forestry action plans in 90 countries.

Yes, but you have to agree we see the sunsets better now

S.B.

Cleaning up pollution. UNEP led a major effort to clean up the Mediterranean Sea. It encouraged adversaries such as Syria and Israel, and Turkey and Greece to work together to clean up beaches. As a result, more than 50 per cent of the previously polluted beaches are now usable.

Light of the World

50

I've got forty-eight hours' leave, Brenda, and the last thing I want to play is 'Piggy in the Middle'!

Protecting consumers' health. To ensure the safety of food sold in the market place, UN agencies have established standards for over 200 food commodities and safety limits for more than 3,000 food contaminants.

52

Of course, these days we're very conservation-minded — but we're also mindful that it pays to advertise!

Reducing fertility rates. The UN Population Fund (UNFPA), through its family planning programmes, has enabled people to make informed choices, and consequently given families, and especially women, greater control over their lives. As a result, women living in developing countries are having fewer children – from 6 births per woman in the 1960s to 3.5 today. In the 1960s only 10 per cent of the world's families were using effective methods of family planning. The number now stands at 55 per cent.

Fighting drug abuse. The UN International Drugs Control Programme (UNDCP) has worked to reduce demand for illicit drugs, suppress drug-trafficking, and has helped farmers to reduce their economic reliance on growing narcotic crops by shifting farm production towards other dependable sources of income.

The council are very environmentally friendly — for every new addict on this estate, they plant a tree...

Improving global trade relations. The UN Conference on Trade and Development (UNCTAD) has worked to obtain special trade preferences for developing countries to export their products to developed countries. It has also negotiated international commodities agreements to ensure fair prices for developing countries. And through the General Agreement on Tariffs and Trade (GATT), which has now been supplanted by the World Trade Organization (WTO), the United Nations has supported trade liberalization, that will increase economic development opportunities in developing countries.

Trouble wid picking up fares from those guys is you spend half your time at the Bureau de Change...

Promoting economic reform. Together with the World Bank and the International Monetary Fund, the United Nations has helped many countries improve their economic management, offered training for government finance officials, and provided financial assistance to countries experiencing temporary balance-of-payment difficulties.

There I was with this beautiful princess, and I was just turning into a handsome prince
when the pesticides in the water gummed up the works

Promoting workers' rights. The International Labour Organization (ILO) has worked to
guarantee freedom of the right to association, the right to organize, collective bargaining, the
rights of indigenous and tribal peoples, promote employment and equal remuneration and
has sought to eliminate discrimination and child labour. And by setting safety standards, ILO
has helped reduce the toll of work-related accidents.

Next door are staging a mass trespass again

58

Corporal punishment? No, I'm into tree conservation

Introducing improved agricultural techniques and reducing costs. With assistance from the Food and Agricultural Organization (FAO) that has resulted in improved crop yields, Asian rice farmers have saved $12 million on pesticides, and governments over $150 million a year on pesticide subsidies.

Alternative Crops

GREETINGS FROM Gus

Promoting stability and order in the world's oceans. Through three international conferences, the third lasting more than nine years, the United Nations has spearheaded an international effort to promote a comprehensive global agreement for the protection, preservation and peaceful development of the oceans. The UN Convention on the Law of the Sea, which came into force in 1994, lays down rules for the determination of national maritime jurisdiction, navigation on the high seas, rights and duties of coastal and other states, obligation to protect and preserve the maritime environment, cooperation in the conduct of marine scientific research and preservation of living resources.

60

Of course they all know that we're completely impartial — why else would both sides keep shooting at us?

Improving air and sea travel. UN agencies have been responsible for setting safety standards for sea and air travel. The efforts of the International Civil Aviation Organization (ICAO) have contributed to making air travel the safest mode of transportation. To wit: in 1947, when 9 million travelled, 590 were killed in aircraft accidents; in 1993 the number of deaths was 936 out of the 1.2 billion airline passengers. Over the last two decades, pollution from tankers has been reduced by as much as 60 per cent thanks to the work of the International Maritime Organization (IMO).

Lifeline UN50

Protecting intellectual property. The World Intellectual Property Organization (WIPO) provides protection for new inventions and maintains a register of nearly three million national trademarks. Through treaties, it also protects the works of artists, composers and authors worldwide. WIPO's work makes it easier and less costly for individuals and enterprises to enforce their property rights. It also broadens the opportunity to distribute new ideas and products without relinquishing control over the property rights.

And what if the Author considers it a breach of copyright — where does that leave us?

Eurocats

Promoting the free flow of information. To allow all people to obtain information that is free of censorship and culturally unbiased, UNESCO has provided aid to develop and strengthen communication systems, established news agencies and supported an independent press.

Improving global communications. The Universal Postal Union (UPU) has maintained and regulated international mail delivery. The International Telecommunications Union (ITU) has coordinated use of the radio spectrum, promoted cooperation in assigning positions for stationary satellites, and established international standards for communications, thereby ensuring the unfettered flow of information around the globe.

Empowering the voiceless. UN-sponsored international years and conferences have caused governments to recognize the needs and contributions of groups usually excluded from decision-making, such as the ageing, children, youth, homeless, and disabled people.

It's a disaster! Those poor people in the ski-resorts!

66

It's shocking and distressing — those boxes aren't recycled

Establishing 'children as a zone of peace'. From El Salvador to Lebanon, Sudan to former Yugoslavia, UNICEF pioneered the establishment of 'Days of Tranquillity' and the opening of 'Corridors of Peace' to provide vaccines and other assistance desperately needed by children caught in armed conflict.

It's peace, Jim, but not as we know it — as usual!

Generating worldwide commitment in support of the needs of children. Through UNICEF's efforts, the Convention on the Rights of the Child entered into force as international law in 1990 and had become law in 166 countries by the end of September 1994; following the 1990 World Summit for Children convened by UNICEF, more than 150 governments have committed to reaching over 20 specific measurable goals to radically improve children's lives by the year 2000.

KUT-UPS

It's another disturbing consequence of acid rain — none of us can yodel any more

You're right — they *are* exhaust fumes

Improving education in developing countries. As a direct result of the efforts of UN agencies, over 60 per cent of adults in developing countries can now read and write, and 80 per cent of children in these countries attend school.

Mark you, it's only a gut feeling, but I don't think that this is the time for maintaining a high profile...

Improving literacy for women. Programmes aimed at promoting education and advancement for women helped raise the female literacy rate in developing countries from 36 per cent in 1970 to 56 per cent in 1990.

72

I think that covers our policy on pollution and the environment

Safeguarding and preserving historic cultural and architectural sites. Ancient monuments in 81 countries including Greece, Egypt, Italy, Indonesia and Cambodia, have been protected through the efforts of UNESCO, and international conventions have been adopted to preserve cultural property.

Give me a call sometime — I'm in the Book

74

We've been called in to keep Thatcher and Major apart

Facilitating academic and cultural exchanges. The United Nations, through UNESCO and the United Nations University (UNU), have encouraged scholarly and scientific cooperation, networking of institutions and promotion of cultural expressions, including those of minorities and indigenous people.

Look, d'you want to remain an undiscovered species all your life?

The Nobel Peace Prize has been awarded five times to the United Nations and its organizations

1954 Office of the United Nations High Commissioner for Refugees, Geneva, for its assistance to European refugees

1965 United Nations Children's Fund (UNICEF), for its work in helping save the lives of the world's children

1969 International Labour Organization (ILO), Geneva, for its progress in establishing workers' rights and protections

1981 Office of the United Nations High Commissioner for Refugees, Geneva, for its assistance to Asian refugees

1988 United Nations Peacekeeping Forces, for their peacekeeping operations

The Prize was also awarded to:

1945   Cordel Hull, U.S., ex-Secretary of State, for his leadership in establishing the UN

1949   Lord John Boyd Orr, United Kingdom, first Director-General of the Food and Agricultural Organization

1950   Ralph Bunche, U.S., UN Mediator in Palestine (1948), for his leadership in the armistice agreements signed in 1949 by Israel, Egypt, Jordan, Lebanon, Syria

1957   Lester Pearson, Canada, ex-Secretary of State, President 7th Session of the UN General Assembly, for a lifetime of work for peace and for leading UN efforts to resolve the Suez Canal Crisis

1961   Dag Hammarskjöld, Sweden, Secretary-General of the UN, for his work in helping settle the Congo Crisis

1974   Sean MacBride, Ireland, UN Commissioner for Namibia

For Peace and Justice in a Sustainable World...

If you want to ensure a better, more equitable world and change public misconceptions and negative attitudes on critical issues affecting the international community, then join an organization where your views really count.

Since 1945, the United Nations Association of Great Britain and Northern Ireland has played a significant role in seeking to develop this country's contribution to international cooperation. A voluntary non-government membership organization, it is uniquely concerned with the many interrelated issues that contribute to the future well-being of our world.

As a member you will join others − people from the complete spectrum of society − with similiar internationalist views, to promote the ideals of the UN Charter through educational programmes and actively campaigning for:

- an agenda for peace through the development and introduction of UN conflict-avoidance and peace-keeping initiatives;
- the development of a sustainable and environmentally safe world by governments and people in cooperation with the UN's Commission on Sustainable Development through the implementation of the internationally agreed Agenda 21;
- human rights for all peoples;
- justice for refugees.

Important elements of the role of the United Nations are to help:

- persuade our government to embrace whole-heartedly every opportunity to enhance international cooperation and understanding;
- ensure that the UN is central to British foreign policy and that our government's actions are consistent with UN resolutions;
- make an informed and considered contribution to the on-going debate on the structure and policies required to ensure the UN's even greater effectiveness in the twenty-first century.

You can join one of our network of branches where you will become involved with the current major issues and further the understanding of international concerns within the community — both at the local and national level.

And at the international level we are linked with other United Nations Associations in more than 80 member states around the world. Collectively we have consultative status with the UN Economic and Social Council — giving our membership a real and significant voice at the heart of the forum where governments make decisions which affect all our lives.

The United Nations Association International Service, our international aid section, sends project workers to developing countries to provide practical help; and we have, over the years, raised more than £2 million to support humanitarian aid programmes for the United Nations High Commissioner for Refugees, the United Nations Children's Fund (UNICEF), the World Health Organization and the World Food Programme.

So if you are committed to the ideals of the United Nations Charter, make your thoughts count — join the United Nations Association now and add your voice and actions to ensure a better, peaceful future for our world.

For further information contact:
The United Nations Association
3 Whitehall Court
London SW1A 2EL

Telephone 0171 930 2931